YOUR KNOWLEDGE HAS VALUE

Internet of Things. Qualitative Aspects of Concept and Implications in the Educational Field With Special Reference to India

Lovish Raheja
MOHIT DIXIT

Bibliographic information published by the German National Library:

The German National Library lists this publication in the National Bibliography; detailed bibliographic data are available on the Internet at http://dnb.dnb.de.

ISBN: 9783346637543
This book is also available as an ebook.

© GRIN Publishing GmbH
Nymphenburger Straße 86
80636 München

Print and binding: Books on Demand GmbH, Norderstedt, Germany
Printed on acid-free paper from responsible sources.

The present work has been carefully prepared. Nevertheless, authors and publishers do not incur liability for the correctness of information, notes, links and advice as well as any printing errors.

GRIN web shop: https://www.grin.com/document/1191298

INTERNET OF THINGS: QUALITATIVE ASPECTS OF CONCEPT AND IMPLICATIONS IN EDUCATIONAL FIELD WITH SPECIAL REFERENCE TO INDIA

MOHIT DIXIT[1] and LOVISH RAHEJA[2]

1. Department of Education, Parishkar College of Global Excellence, Shipra Path, Mansarovar, Jaipur, affiliated to the University of Rajasthan, Jaipur.
2. Department of Education, Parishkar College of Global Excellence, affiliated to the University of Rajasthan, Jaipur.

Table of contents

1. ABSTRACT 3

2. INTRODUCTION 3

3. LITERATURE REVIEW 4

4. OBJECTIVE OF THE STUDY 8

5. RESEARCH METHODOLOGY 9

6. CONCEPT OF IOT 9

7. PRESENT STATUS OF IOT IN INDIA 11

8. NEED OF IOT IN EDUCATION IN INDIA 12

9. CHALLENGES IN ADOPTION OF BEST PRACTICES OF IOT 15

10. RECOMMENDATIONS (ANALYTIC APPROACH TO THE CHALLENGES)...........................17

11. CONCLUSIVE REMARKS 18

12. REFERENCES: 20

INTERNET OF THINGS: QUALITATIVE ASPECTS OF CONCEPT AND IMPLICATIONS IN EDUCATIONAL FIELD WITH SPECIAL REFERENCE TO INDIA

1. ABSTRACT

The Internet of Things (IoT) is transforming the modern world. Presently, every field of life is being considered under the scope of IoT. Education is one of them and the field to be explored the most as education leads the world and so the technological inputs in it. The purpose of this study is to qualitatively evaluate the concept of IoT and discover the potential areas of implementation of it in the educational scenario in Indian perspectives specifically. IoT is basically connecting the things with the internet for the major purpose of communication of information and execution of defined programs. India is going to make huge progress in this field as per the official estimations but the educational field in India still lacks many of the advancements which have been made recently and which are successfully working in the other fields. Connecting the leaners and faculties to a smart AI-systems is one of the key ideas to be focused on. The entire education system which consists of administrative processes, learning and teaching activities, evaluation methods etc. may be transformed through it. Through the specific approach to the Indian context, we have tried to identify the challenges of IoT in the country such as high expenses due to a large number of students, privacy and ethical issues, lack of trained workforce etc. Further, we have tried to give some recommendations to face and tackle the challenges in an efficient manner, the implementation of which may lead to the success of IoT in the educational field as well.

Keywords: IoT, Educational field, Challenges, Implementation in India

2. INTRODUCTION

We are living in a world where science and technology leads. But when it comes to the implementation of technologies in the country like India and that too in the field of education is a great matter of concern. It is known to all of us that the way we teach today in the classes is not up to the mark of current technological achievements. The way we are teaching in generals like the use of chalk-duster and green-board could be used even two centuries ago. This tells us how we lag behind in the educational field. There are very fewer institutions trying to follow the latest technological trends. The main thing is education is a basic right and to make its approach universal, we cut down all the possible infrastructural costs specifically discussing with reference to India. So, the main problem, in general, turns out to be the cost of the technologies.

The study is focused on the educational field as we realize that the change in the educational field is to lead the change in the mindsets of the people. The technological inputs in education may unblock the rigidity of minds, open the world for the people and build the capacity of thinking out of the box which ultimately leads to the sustainable growth of the country. The fields like computer-related technologies also contribute their significant part in sustainability which is essential to keep in mind.

This study aims at recommending the universalization of the internet in the educational field confronting possible major issues and problems in its implementation and proposing well-executable solutions. At first, the concept of the Internet of Things (IoT) and present status in the country have been evaluated. Then the specific approach to education has been adopted. The need and challenges have been identified and possible recommendations are given.

Actually, presently available pieces of literature do not seem to be counted against the problems of the implementation of IoT in Indian perspective. This has been done in this study with the help of ground-level observation and understanding of the scenarios.

The approach to the study has been developed with the help of secondary literature available on the subject but the study owns novelty through its analysis part. By analysing the issues and problems the study develops the solutions to the problems. Hence, overall, the study focuses on the development of IoT in the educational field. Researching the applications of IoT and planning for proper execution is the main goal of this study.

3. LITERATURE REVIEW

Pruet et al. in their study titled *'Exploring the Internet of "Educational Things" (IoET) in rural underprivileged areas' (2015)* have particularly discussed he development and design for the Internet of Educational Things (IoET). The study holds a specific approach by limiting its criteria to rural under-privileged primary school learning activities in northern Thailand. In the paper, firstly, the analyses of the wide application of IoT in education and discussion of economic aspects have been made and then the primary project-based study is illustrated through which an in-depth approach to the application of IoT has been shown. This study is complete in itself starting from the basics and comprehensive view, the study ends up with advance and specific results.

Vienna, Manjulatha & Soumya in their study titled *'A Study on the Integration of IoT and Cloud Computing for Education System' (2016)* discuss the potential benefits of the integration of IoT with cloud computing to the education system. IoT is basically related to linking physical objects to the internet making them communicate to each other without human interaction whereas cloud computing with regard to IoT is related to the processing of the data collected by those physical objects functioning as sensors. The study discusses the need for their integration, four major pillars of IoT, key factors affecting the successful implementation of IoT in the educational field. Individual differences are one of the greatest challenges in the educational field and this integration may work as a boon here. The four major pillars are people, process, data and things and the factors affecting the implementation of IoT are data integrity, security and favourable education policies. The potential applications of this integration which have been discussed are enhanced learning experiences and outcomes, improved operational efficiency, designing safer campuses.

Overall, the study holds a wide scope discussing essential aspects related to the applications of IoT. The study is broad in nature and does not belong to any region-specific but still, it is an important guide to understand the related concept and theories.

Aldowah et al., in their study titled *'Internet of Things in Higher Education: A Study on Future Learning' (2017)* introduces the basic components of IoT giving the preliminary idea of the concept to the readers. IoT components are majorly divided into three parts- hardware, middleware and presentation. Hardware includes sensors, actuators and tools for embedded communication purpose. Middleware consists of on-demand storage and data analytic tools. Presentation part includes visualization tools, easy interpretive equipment which can be accessed and designed for wide applications. There are several approaches for efficient communication. Wi-Fi is one of the most popular and best as per the power-per-bit transmission efficiency. IoT has potential usages in equipping any device with sensor technologies. Further, the authors have introduced the concept of the digital campus, which is extremely useful in the present era. They have basically recommended the integration of highly advanced technologies to the physical campuses.

Our approach is little different to some extent as we emphasize the least physical infrastructural cost and creating a virtual environment as much as possible considering related financial and security issues. Such an environment will also foster research activities and will ultimately bring educational quality to a new level. Integration of IoT to the education may affect almost all the aspects of education including administration, entrance process, classroom teaching etc. So, this paper gives an idea of the application of IoT to higher education but does not seem to have a specific approach. This study is a comprehensive review providing with the broader applications of IoT in higher education.

Bhatt & Bhatt in their study titled *'IoT Techniques to Nurture Education Industry: Scope & Opportunities' (2017)* have surveyed the different procedures utilized for quality e-learning purposes powered by IoT technology. The paper coincides with the study by Venna et al. (2016) discussed above at many points. The key factors for successful implementation of IoT and pillars of IoT are the common points. The study provides a comprehensive list of wide application areas of IoT. Various aspects like E-education, E-lab, virtual research offices with blended realistic experiences have been discussed in the paper. Possible obvious future works have also been illustrated. This paper gives an idea of initiation of our study by taking broader perspectives of IoT application to research but considering it in the Indian context.

In a review article written by *Maksimović* titled *'IoT Concept Application in Educational Sector Using Collaboration' (2017)* have analysed the ways to achieve positively transformed educational practices with the help of modern Information and Communication Technologies (ICTs) particularly IoT. Alongside, their potential to contribute to a socially and economically sustainable educational environment have also been discussed. The author has also emphasised on the need for collaboration among all stakeholders for optimum outcomes. The author has deeply illustrated IoT and collaboration symbiotic approach for improving educational quality. This gives the learner social, academic and psychological benefits along with assessment advantages. Also, potential improvements in the role and skills of the teachers by the betterment in reflective dialogues, observational learning to teach, collaborative professional activities etc. have been thoroughly reviewed. The positive impacts on the educational environment would be reduced cost to pay to extra manpower implies that more and more to be invested on skill development of the teachers and other staff, maintaining cleanliness in the terms of clean energy production, less energy consumption, less waste generation etc., better and safer infrastructure etc.

Hence, overall, the study evaluates the need for IoT in present era especially emphasising on a collaborative approach, which is extremely commendable. This would help students be better

6

learners and humans and teaching fraternity become more skilful and better persons in life ultimately nurturing and fostering a healthier educational environment.

Shrinath et al. in their study titled *'IOT Application in Education' (2017)* illustrate the concept of smart education which includes smart teaching, smart classrooms and smart learning through IoT, and smart vehicle management techniques with the application of IoT. They conclude that IoT would be helpful for better learning experiences, easier handling of complex administrative systems by the participating stakeholders, increasing reliability of the system, and building safer and securer campuses.

This study gives a good idea of the potential usages of IoT in the field of education. Learning is, of course, the most important part of education which is enhanced through IoT. But the educational institutes have a broader framework consisting of complex administrative structures including vehicle management which is also given ample space in this study. This study also does not hold a specific approach to any region. Our study is different in this manner providing a specific approach to the Indian context.

Pandharkar & Suryawanshi in their study titled *'Generalized Educational Model Based on Internet of Things for Educational Institutes'* (2018) recommend a generalized model for the transformation of the educational system for essential quality enhancements. They discuss majorly five areas of usage of IoT which are: Connecting classrooms to the outside world, improving the learning process, improving teaching process, bettering administrative structures, and ensuring security and safety of the student.

This study discusses various aspects of IoT for education in a qualitative way. Our study is also supposed to be qualitative in nature. But again, this study also does not seem to fit any particular regional context which has been tried in our study.

Das, Hazari & Karmakar in their study titled *'IoT in Modern Day Education: A Study' (2018)* discuss various techniques of IoT for modern-day education system including Radio Frequency Identification (RFID), cloud storage, smart classrooms consisting of smart surveillance systems, smart attendance and different types of sensor technologies. Also, IoT enabled e-learning which helps to create an international community of student in and out of the classroom has been discussed. A smart library which may use Wi-Fi-based Local Positioning System (LPS), Near Field Communication (NFC) for finding the position of the books and also for authentication purposes. Further, the study discusses different network protocols in IoT and then provides with a comprehensive comparison among various techniques of IoT and among applications of IoT discussing the socio-economic applicability of the same.

Hence, overall, the study comprehensively evaluates the application of IoT in the education system. It also gives an idea of the possible issues related to the applicability in regional context classified as urban and rural areas. This study provides a guide for the limiting depth of the study to make our study useful and accomplishable in a timely manner.

In a study conducted by IoT Panel of The Institution of Engineering and Technology titled *'Smart Education – Making education Efficient, Affordable and Reachable for India' (2018)* various aspects of smart education have been discussed. In this study, the growing economic share in the field of smart education has been illustrated. They have recommended three major points to transform the education system with the help of IoT technologies which are: Government to play an active role in the ground-level implementation of these technologies by providing incentives, forming norms to rapidly adopt the technological changes, encouraging private enterprises and start-ups etc., IoT solution and service providers companies to work on reducing the cost of the technology adoption so to make it affordable, and educational institutes to analyse the trends and patterns of modern technologies to maintain best practices in their campuses. The study majorly aims at raising awareness related to the technology, highlighting key challenges and giving fruitful recommendations for the successful implementation of IoT for smart education. The study describes almost all possible stakeholders of smart education deeply.

This position paper analyses the need and applicability of smart education through IoT in Indian regional context. The study is useful in the manner that it takes the notice of specific socio-economic context India with the help of which it gives practical suggestions.

4. OBJECTIVE OF THE STUDY

To study the concept and implications of the Internet of Things (IoT) in the educational field with special reference to India.

RESEARCH QUESTIONS

1) What is the concept of IoT?
2) What is the present status of IoT in the Indian context?
3) What is the need for IoT in the educational field?

4) What are the challenges in adopting the best technological practices in the educational field in India?

5) What are the practical recommendations for the successful implementation of IoT in the educational field?

5. RESEARCH METHODOLOGY

This research is basically a literature survey with in-depth analysis of the subject. Therefore, it is dependent mainly on secondary data. The secondary resources used are believed to be reliable and valid across the globe. They are basically reputed journals, proceedings of international conferences, and various reports prepared by prestigious institutions etc. The resources are collected from various databases such as google scholar, different search engines and global research platforms etc.

The framework of the study is explained in the following flow-diagram:

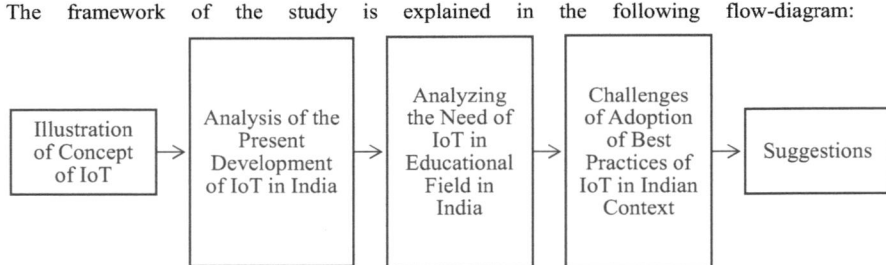

Fig.1: Framework of the Study

6. CONCEPT OF IOT

IoT refers to the internet of things. The term is somewhat related to the ability of network devices to sense and collect data from the world and then share the data on Internet where its processing and utilization is done for various purposes (Sharma & Tiwari, 2015). As we all know that internet has brought a huge impact in our lives and the internet of things, in a farther step, has spread the applicability of Internet across many more objects than laptops, computers and smartphones etc. IoT is a step towards making real-world things intelligent so that they can take their decisions by themselves (Mohammed & Ahmed, 2017).

Jun (2014) traces the origin of IoT in an article written in 1982 by Carnegie Mellon University Computer Science Department titled "The 'Only' Coke Machine on the Internet" in which the author told about the functioning of the internet-connected coke machine. In 1992, the University of Cambridge with a remote procedure call (RPC) mechanism managed to connect a coffee machine to the internet. Later on, many pieces of research came in the picture through which this field broadened.

The term 'Internet of Things' was first used by Kevin Ashton, a member of the Radio Frequency Identification Development Community in 1999 (Patel & Patel, 2016). Now we actually need to know what Radio Frequency Identification (RFID) refers to. RFID systems are automatic technologies which identify objects, collect desired data and control individual target through radio frequency (Jia et al., 2012).

Hence, if we try to reiterate the concept of IoT in our own words: The main idea behind IoT is to make real-world objects smarter. Smartness that is not to be limited till smartphones or computers but to generalize it as much as possible. If we observe the machines or any object around us from fan to almirah, automating everything comes under the scope of IoT. For example, your fan automatically switches off, when you cross the boundary of your room and your almirah automatically opens when you come near the almirah recognizing your identity.

The term is not to be confused with the Internet of Everything (IoE) which is a next step ahead. IoT is only concerned about physical objects but IoE has four major pillars: people, process, data and things (Chauhan and Jain, 2019). It involves people to people, machine to machine and people to machine communication (Miraz and Ali, 2015).

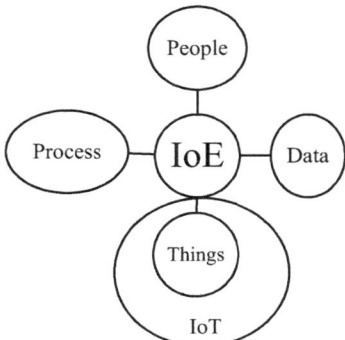

Fig.2: Concept Diagram Representing the Difference Between IoE & IoT

It is now clear that IoT may have numerous applications which cannot be listed completely as making any machine which can sense and act according to the situation comes under the scope of IoT. So, now there is another term which is to understand well in this context which is Artificial Intelligence commonly known as AI. Though there is a clear intersection between these two. IoT is basically based on Machine to Machine Communication whereas AI is related to make machines intelligent and thoughtful like humans and even better in some cases. Hence AI is not limited to the machine to machine communication but it also involves people to machine communication as well. (Difference between IoT and AI, n.d.).

So, till now we have understood the important terms which are often confused with IoT. Some of the essential application of IoT involves smart transportation, environmental monitoring, manufacturing, medical and health care services, home automation, energy management, media, entertainment, agriculture, security etc. (Reddy & Mohan, 2017). Also, the application which this paper is focused on is education. This application can be thought of by studying different components of education. Administrative activities, teaching-learning process, evaluation, infrastructural development all may be hugely impacted by the advancements in IoT.

The admission process can be ratified through IoT. Entries through digital documents, data collection and operation can be automated through IoT technologies. Development of smart-classrooms equipped with smart desks, smart boards, different types of sensors etc. is IoT induced. Further online evaluation, smart assessments etc. can be achieved with IoT. Also, we can have security enhancement operations through IoT. Security involves not only the security of campus but also of teachers and learner, even time to time mental and physical health assessments are also possible with this advanced technological paradigm.

7. PRESENT STATUS OF IOT IN INDIA

The development of IoT is being rapidly encouraged in India. According to COMSNETS (cited in Yadav, Mittal & Yadav, 2018) report in 2015 Indian government has planned to spend ₹7060 crores (US $0.927 billion) in IoT for developing 100 smart cities. This expenditure is mainly aimed at better government services, technological advancements, raising the living standards of people, better environment. Though, the results have not been observed yet. The 'Digital India Program' seems quite successful to encourage digitalization across the country, but the use of IoT is still limited. Fortunately, India seems to be heading in the right direction. By 2020, the IoT market in India was expected to grow to US $15 billion from $5.6 billion in 2018, but this growth must have been affected by the present COVID-19 pandemic. But India still lags behind, if we see from global perspectives. Though, the NASSCOM report (cited in Rishi & Saluja, n.d.) says India is going to be a front runner in the adoption of IoT in Asia Pacific region with Compound Annual Growth Rate of 62% of Indian IoT market and would reach US $9 billion in 2020. IoT connections are expected to grow with the growth rate of 137%. Globally, expenditure on IoT is the highest in the field of manufacturing but in India, it is highest in utilities followed by manufacturing, transport and logistics, automotive industries, healthcare and so on. As per the distribution provided in the 'Future of IoT', there is very less expenditure on the consumer IoT as compared to the global share. This expenditure is important from the perspectives of education. Government of India has taken many important initiatives in the direction of the development of IoT technologies. Launching draft IoT policy 2016, National Digital Communications Policy 2018, Smart Cities Mission 2015, IoT centre of excellence by NASSCOM, DEITY and ERNET are the recent steps. According to a study by Deloitte (cited in ASMA Content lab, n.d.), the number of total IoT devices in India is around 60 million which is expected to increase to 1.9 billion by 2020.

Therefore, we observe that there are high possibilities of development of IoT technologies in India and optimistically, India is going to lead in this field growth rate-wise. But the expenditure on education is still very less. In India, there are very few companies presently aimed at the goal of providing IoT solutions for smart education purposes which are countable on fingers. Now, before going to illustrate such challenges we would light upon the need of IoT in Indian perspective.

8. NEED OF IOT IN EDUCATION IN INDIA

The following concerns specify the needs of IoT in education in India:

Low Teacher-Student Ratio and Concerns of Quality

India is a highly populous country. Due to this fact, India mostly lags behind in essential facilities when talked in terms of ratios with respect to the population such as doctor-patient ratio, student-teacher ratio, unemployability etc. These problems need smart solutions which are only possible with the help of technological inputs. Especially, when we talk about education, quality education is also a sustainable development goal. Along with this, quality education is a fundamental right and as it is known that teacher-student ratio is very low in India which implies that individual attention to the progress of each student is not possible. If we see in the higher education segment the ratio is 1:24 (Indo-Asian News Service, 2019) which is lower than several countries including Brazil and China.

Individual differences matter a lot in the educational field. The aim of education is to develop the student holistically which cannot be fulfilled without giving attention to each individual that is the point where technology helps. Technology is to be taken as a supportive infrastructure for the teachers to help them achieve their desired goal of behavioural change (learning) in the students. Individual tracking of every student is possible through inputs of IoT technologies. The teacher can track the progress of each individual with IoT, hence, can ensure the development of all in an optimum manner.

Designing virtual science labs is also being done as a part of the transformation. Ramlowat and Patnayak (2019) have mentioned the special use of IoT in educational field which involves application in computer science education, smart books, augmented reality or mobile computing, creating hyper situations, medical education with IoTFLIP, manpower training using HOPPING and ESIC and various other implications in other educational fields. Hence, quality education concerns may be solved to a good extent through these technological inputs.

The aspect which has been discussed is related to facilitate the teaching-learning process but the application of IoT is not limited to that only. IoT can be also used for various other purposes. As an education system is not merely teaching-learning, so we need to consider many other aspects as well.

Tackling with Issues Related to Corruption

In India, there are vast and complex educational structures which cannot be regulated by the external assessment bodies in the best possible manner. Technological inputs may help here, especially, the use of IoT. Smart surveillance systems such as one mentioned by Gunnemeda et al. (2018) using Raspberry Pi Single Board Computer (SBC) with Wi-Fi network connectivity., attendance automation technology as one illustrated by B.M. et al. (2019) using Radio Frequency Identification Technology (RFID) and Raspberry pi 3 etc. can be maintained and monitored through IoT applications. Further, encouraging open data movement as mentioned by Exner (2014) for smart cities can also be deployed for administrative implications in the educational field. This would bring transparency in the whole system which would help in the extinction of corruption.

Saving Time, Maintaining Discipline and Managing Administration

Indian educational institutions are "overloaded" if said frankly. For such a dense populous country, this is obvious. But this often causes management failure due to which the students become undisciplined as proper monitoring structures are not there. One breaks the law and not get even realized of its mistake as one cannot be blamed without evidence or monitoring. Applications of such systems would discourage the discipline-brokers. Also, record maintenance, account management can be worked out in minimal time with these IoT applications.

Environmental Need

As it is well known that the whole world is suffering from the environmental issue is severe in India. Though the present pandemic (COVID-19) has forced many countries to impose lockdown due to which environmental recovery have been observed but if such technological inputs are not adopted, our environment would degrade as earlier and educational activities have a lot to do with the development of the sense of environmental care which can be fostered through green inputs in education itself. From environmental perspectives, the aim of green education can be accomplished through IoT technologies. Also, energy demands can also be accomplished with the help of advanced IoT technologies equipped with renewable and cleaner energy sources for optimisation purposes. Various control and optimization techniques have been reported by Raheja (2019) in this regard. Also, Tabuenca et al. (2020) insist on the agronomical activities using smart IoT sensors for improving soil quality, optimizing water usage, etc. and they focus on its application in the educational institutions to foster awareness related to environmental health. Moreover, security enhancements can be done through various IoT technologies, identifying unauthorised persons through RFID technology is possible for avoiding leakage of offline and online question papers. There are innumerable such applications of IoT.

Practical and Laboratory Experience in Open and Distance Learning

The set-up of virtual laboratories and practical experience is a big challenge with respect to Open and Distance learning. IoT has fortunately many solutions of the problem such as one mentioned by Bajracharya and Blackford (2018) as content management tool.

9. CHALLENGES IN ADOPTION OF BEST PRACTICES OF IOT

There are many challenges in the practical implementation of IoT on ground-level. Firstly, the challenges cited in various pieces of literature have been provided with.

Banafa (2017) has divided the challenges facing IoT into 3 parts: technology, business and society. This study provides a holistic view of the challenges of IoT applicable in all the fields. Some of these challenges are as follows:

Security

Security of devices which are connected to the internet has always been one of the major concerns. The intelligence of physical objects we are talking may get affected by the hacking, which in turn may also deteriorate the objective to be achieved.

Connectivity

Connecting so many devices is going to be a great challenge. Presently a centralized paradigm is being followed which is sufficient as per the no. of present devices. But later, there are going to be several issues which are being thought of before practical implementational actions.

Compatibility and Standards

The field of IoT is developing in many different directions and many technologies are competing to become the standard. This will cause difficulties and the use of extra equipment and programs to function. Cloud services are non-unified and also, there is no standard Machine to Machine Communication (M2M) protocols, these issues raise compatibility issues for maintenance of software and hardware.

Evolution of a Standard Business Model and Requirement of Liberal Approach

There is an essential need for the evolution of new standard business model for IoT which leads the way of implementation of these technologies at ground-level. The liberal approach by regulatory bodies is also needed because strict laws at initial stages are a hindrance in the optimum development of these technologies and restrict the speed of development.

Societal Issues

Society is a dynamic structure and so the needs of the society. As the technologies progress, the demands of the societies change automatically. IoT devices are made for long-term usages, so this is a big concern. Further, the cost of IoT devices is going to fall as the trend shows

(Leonard, 2019). This would create problems in the implementation of these technologies at the initial level considering human psychology. Actually, this may also cause issues related to confidence on products which may hinder in achieving the full potential of IoT.

Some other challenges are to make sure the availability of reliable Wi-Fi connections which is a big security concern, management of IoT devices in a manner that the availability and reliability of these devices for all users are well maintained and expensiveness in the present scenario is also a challenge, though time and technological progress would tackle with it (Gul et al., 2017).

Now, based on the ground-level observations, we have identified some other challenges which are:

The attitude of Management Personnel

It is seen that management personnel are often rigid and resisting to change and do not easily adapt the technological changes which are the need of time. According to us, this is the primary requirement for the adoption of change. Hence, developing a positive attitude for growth according to the time is one of the biggest challenges.

Tech-friendliness of Teachers and Non-teaching Staff

Being in the field of education, it is essential to be tech-friendly of teachers and non-teaching staff especially when the institution is aimed at adopting innovative technological practices. Teachers who are unaware of the latest aspects of technology do not let their student learn in the best possible manner which is a big hindrance in its conceptual progress. Non-teaching staff such as administrative persons and computer experts also play a big role here such as in making the learning content interactive and interesting, also making the administrative activities run smoothly using the technology.

Students' Interest

This fact may seem strange but this is reality. It is seen that intelligent students resist technical changes many times, maybe because of their concept about learning which they think is about increasing memory power and use of IoT moves the student away from rote learning which is the need of modern times, so a great focus should be on changing students' perception about learning which is also a big challenge.

The requirement of Separate Infrastructure

To equip present institutions with advanced technologies like IoT, separate rooms like server rooms, and facilities are required to smoothly manage all the operations. This is also a challenge to face.

Power Management System

India is not a country with 24 x 7 electric supply. There is a lack in supply of the electricity demand. But inputs of technologies would require a full-time power supply. The challenge becomes severe when rural areas of the country are concerned. So, this big challenge is also needed to be solved in a well-managed manner.

10.RECOMMENDATIONS (ANALYTIC APPROACH TO THE CHALLENGES)

- Security issues are subject to technological progress. Therefore, investments should be made in 'Research and Development for IoT Security'. Also, there is a need to deploy proper norms rigorously concerning network security and privacy issues.
- Centralized systems of IoT management are not going to be very useful in future. So, Fog Computing provides a solution to this problem. Fog computing is defined as *"a geographically distributed computing architecture with a resource pool consists of one or more ubiquitously connected heterogeneous (variegated)devices (including edge devices) at the sting of network and not solely seamlessly backed by cloud services, to collaboratively provide elastic computation, storage and communication (and many other new services and tasks) in isolated environments to an outsized scale of purchasers in proximity"*. (Harish et al., 2019). Basically, fog computing is a type of decentralized computing solving the problems of centralization of technological management.
- There is a need of the formation of a chain of governing bodies consisting of computer science expert to ensure proper standards related to the business models and technical management and building standard M2M protocols for smooth implementation of IoT technologies in India.
- The liberal approach in terms of forgiving extra charges, providing subsidies, encouragement of start-ups to evolve and provide innovative approach etc. is needed at the administrative or government level.

- Awareness programs are needed to be run at the ground-level to avoid the misuse and for secure operations of IoT devices. Also, enlightening people with cyber-laws may help a lot.

- A psychological and technical training must be provided to the educational personnel be it teachers or non-teaching staff so to adopt the changes rapidly and to obtain cent-per cent outputs.

- Igniting the interest of students is also important, some seminars can be arranged for this purpose giving them insight technology-based learning so to adopt the changes in a pleasant way.

- The administration and government should provide support to the institutions adopting changes as a need of time in initial stages. Government agencies should also help the institutions in maintaining full-power supply. Availability of inverters or generators can also be ensured. There is another solution to this challenge by adopting green energy solutions. The institutions can be self-dependent for energy supply using solar panels, wind power generations or micro-energy generators for various different applications such as one rotary electromagnetic generator mentioned by Niroomand and Foroughi (2016). Decentralized micro-grids to ensure local power supply is also a good option.

11.CONCLUSIVE REMARKS

This paper aims at studying the concept and implication of the IoT technologies in the Indian education system. A comprehensive survey of literature has been done to identify the limits of research which have taken place hitherto. It can be stated that IoT is basically, the communication technology between machines or in other words IoT is a set of technologies which enable the machine to machine communication without human interaction. Moreover, it is aimed at making things smart and able to take decisions by themselves. Further, the study of the present status of IoT in India gives hopes for speedy development of these technologies in India as India seems to be leading the progress rate in the Asia Pacific region. In the context of the need of IoT in the educational field, low teacher-student ratio, low quality of education, increasing corruption, mismanaged administration, environmental concerns are the factors which create of the need of these technological inputs in the educational field. During the identification of challenges various issues like security, connectivity, compatibility, standardization, societal values, attitudes of students, teacher, and non-teaching staff and finally, lack of proper training and knowledge programs came into view solutions for which are recommended accordingly such as investments in R&D, running awareness programs, Fog Computing, psychological and technical training etc. are recommended. Overall, the paper aims at creating awareness regarding the implementation of IoT technologies in education for quality enhancement as a major need.

12.REFERENCES:

1) Aldowah, H., Rehman, S., Ghazal, S., & Umar, I.N. (2017, September 1). Internet of Things in Higher Education: A Study on Future Learning. *Journal of Physics: Conference Series, 892,* 01-10.

2) B M, Madhu & Kanagotagi, K. & Devansh. (2017). IoT based Automatic Attendance Management System. *International Conference on Current Trends in Computer, Electrical, Electronics and Communication (ICCTCEEC-2017),* 83-86. 10.1109/CTCEEC.2017.8455099.

3) Banafa, A. (2017, March 14). Three Major Challenges Facing IoT (Newsletter). *IEEE Internet of Things.* Retrieved from: https://iot.ieee.org/newsletter/march-2017/three-major-challenges-facing-iot

4) Bhatt, J., & Bhatt, A. (2017). IoT Techniques to Nurture Education Industry: Scope & Opportunities. *International Journal on Emerging Technologies, 8*(1), 128-132.

5) Chauhan, D., & J, J.K. (2019, September). *A Journey from IoT to IoE. International Journal of Innovative Technology and Exploring Engineering (IJITEE), 8*(11), 966-969. 10.35940/ijitee.H7002.0981119

6) Das, A., Hazari, A., & Karmakar, R. (2018, March). IOT IN MODERN DAY EDUCATION: A STUDY. *International Journal of Latest Trends in Engineering and Technology, 10*(1), 331-336.

7) Difference Between IoT and AI (n.d.). *Difference Between.net.* Retrieved from: http://www.differencebetween.net/technology/difference-between-iot-and-ai/

8) Gul, S., Asif, M., Ahmad, S., Yasir, M., Majid, M., & Malik, M.S. (2017, May). A Survey on Role of Internet of Things in Education. *International Journal of Computer Science and Network Security, 17*(5), 159-165.

9) Gunnemeda, L. K., Gadde, S.C., Guduru, H., Devarapalli, M.B., & Peketi, S.K. (2018). IoT Based Smart Surveillance System. *International Journal of Advance Research and Development, 3*(2), 166-171.

10) Harish, G., Nagaraju, S., Harish, B., & Shaik, M. (2019, April). A Review on Fog Computing and its Applications. *International Journal of Innovative Technology and Exploring Engineering (IJITEE), 8*(6C2). ISSN: 2278-3075.

11) Exner, J.P. (2014, May). *Smart Planning and Smart Cities.* Proceedings REAL CORP 2014 Tagungsband, Vienna, Austria, 603-610. ISBN: 978-3-9503110-7-5 (Print).

12) How Internet of Things Is Changing the Landscape of Indian Institutes? (n.d.). Adoption of Social Media in Academia Content Lab. Retrieved from: https://www.asmaindia.in/blog/how-internet-of-things-is-changing-the-landscape-of-indian-institutes/

13) Indo-Asian News Service (2019, July 14). India's student-teacher ratio lowest among compared countries lags behind Brazil and China. *India Today Group*. Retrieved from: https://www.indiatoday.in/education-today/news/story/india-s-student-teacher-ratio-lowest-lags-behind-brazil-and-china-1568695-2019-07-14

14) Jia, X., Feng, Q., Fan, T., & Lei, Q. (2012). *RFID technology and its applications in the Internet of Things (IoT)*. 2012 2nd International Conference on Consumer Electronics, Communications and Networks, CECNet 2012 - Proceedings. 10.1109/CECNet.2012.6201508.

15) Jun, Z. (2014, November 27). *Internet of Things, Disruption or Destruction?* Amsterdam Business School.

16) Leonard, M. (2019, October 14). Declining price of IoT sensors means greater use in manufacturing. *Supply Chain Dive*. Retrieved from: https://www.supplychaindive.com/news/declining-price-iot-sensors-manufacturing/564980/

17) Maksimović, M. (2017). IOT CONCEPT APPLICATION IN EDUCATIONAL SECTOR USING COLLABORATION. *Teaching, Learning and Teacher Education Series, 1*(2), 137-150. 10.22190/FUTLTE1702137M

18) Miraz, M., Ali, M., Excell, P.S., & Picking, R. (2015). A review on the Internet of Things (IoT), Internet of Everything (IoE) and Internet of Nano Things (IoNT). *2015 Internet Technologies and Applications (ITA)*, Wrexham, 219-224.

19) Mohammed, Z.K., & Ahmed, E.S. (2017). Internet of Things Applications, Challenges and Related Future Technologies. *World Scientific News (WSN), 67*(2), 126-148.

20) Niroomand, M., Foroughi, H.R. (2016). A rotary electromagnetic microgenerator for energy harvesting from human motions. *Journal of Applied Research and Technology, 14*(4), 259-267.

21) Pandharkar, M. & Suryawanshi, K. (2018, February). *GENERALIZED EDUCATIONAL MODEL BASED ON INTERNET OF THINGS FOR EDUCATIONAL INSTITUTES*. Proceedings of International Conference on Advances in Computer Technology and Management (ICACTM). ISBN: 978-81-921768-9-5.

22) Patel, K.K., & Patel, S.M. (2016, May). Internet of Things-IoT: Definition, Characteristics, Architecture, Enabling Technologies, Application & Future Challenges. *International Journal of Engineering Science and Computing, 6*(5), 6122-6131. 10.4010/2016.1482

23) Pruet, P., Ang, C.S., Farzin, D., & Chaiwut, N. (2015, June). *Exploring the Internet of "Educational Things" (IoET) in rural underprivileged areas.* 12th International Conference on Electrical Engineering/Electronics, Computer, Telecommunications and Information Technology (ECTI-CON), Hua Hin, Thailand. 10.1109/ECTICon.2015.7207125.

24) Raheja, L. (2019, Number). Power Electronics for Renewable Energy Systems: Current Approaches and Future Prospects. *International Journal of Science, Engineering and Management, 6*(11), 3-7. 01.1617/vol6/iss11/pid28516.

25) Ramlowat, D. D., & Pattanayak, B. K. (2019). Exploring the Internet of Things (IoT) in Education: A Review. *Information Systems Design and Intelligent Applications,* 245-255. 10.1007/978-981-13-3338-5_23

26) Reddy, M.T., & Mohan, R.K. (2017, April). Applications of IoT: A Study. National Conference on Emerging Trends in Computing (NCETC-2K17), Department of Computer Applications, Godavari Institute of Engineering and Technology, Rajahmundry, A.P 7th & 8th April 2017. Special Issue Published in *International Journal of Trend in Research and Development (IJTRD),* 86-87. ISSN: 2394-9333. 10.13140/RG.2.2.27960.60169

27) Rishi, R., & Saluja, R. (n.d.). Future of IoT. Federation of Indian Chambers of Commerce and Industry (FICCI), India.

28) Sharma, V., & Tiwari, R. (2016, February). A review paper on "IoT" & Its Smart Applications. *International Journal of Science, Engineering and Technology Research (IJSETR), 5*(2), 472-476.

29) Shrinath, Vikhyath, Shivani, Sanket, & Shruti (2017). IoT Application in Education. *International Journal of Advanced Research and Development, 2*(6), 20-24.

30) *Smart Education – Making education Efficient, Affordable and Reachable for India* (2018, October). The Institution of Engineering and Technology. Retrieved from: http://iotindiacongress.com/wp-content/uploads/2019/06/Smart-Education.pdf

31) Tabuenca, B., Garcia-Alcantara, V., Gilarranz-Casado, C., & Barrado-Aguirre, S. (2020). Fostering Environmental Awareness with Smart IoT Planters in Campuses. *Sensors, 20*(8), 2227. MDPI AG. 10.3390/s20082227.

32) Venna, A., Manjulatha, B., & Soumya, K. (2016, June). A Study on the Integration of IoT and Cloud Computing for Education System. *International Journal of Innovative Research in Computer and Communication Engineering, 4*(6), 12279-12284. 10.15680/IJIRCCE.2016. 0406280

33) Yadav, P., Mittal, A., & Yadav, H. (2018). *IoT: Challenges and Issues in Indian Perspective.* 2018 3rd International Conference on Internet of Things: Smart Innovation and Usages (IoT-SIU), Bhimtal, 1-5. 10.1109/IoT-SIU.2018.85198.

YOUR KNOWLEDGE HAS VALUE

- We will publish your bachelor's and master's thesis, essays and papers

- Your own eBook and book - sold worldwide in all relevant shops

- Earn money with each sale

Upload your text at www.GRIN.com and publish for free